Pass It On

AFRICAN-AMERICAN POETRY
FOR CHILDREN

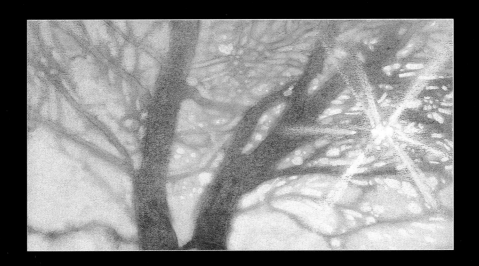

Selected by Wade Hudson
Illustrated by Floyd Cooper

SCHOLASTIC
HARDCOVER

SCHOLASTIC INC.
NEW YORK

—For Mama—
F.C.

—For Ma' Dear, Stephan & Katura—
W.H.

The illustrations for this book were painted in oil wash on board.

The type was set in Cheltenham.

Designed by Cheryl Willis Hudson

Library of Congress Cataloging-in-Publication Data

Pass it on: African-American poetry for children / selected by Wade
  Hudson; illustrated by Floyd Cooper.
        p. cm.
      Summary: An illustrated collection of poetry by such Afro-
American poets as Langston Hughes, Nikki Giovanni, Eloise Greenfield,
and Lucille Clifton.
              ISBN 0-590-45770-5
      1. Children's poetry, American–Afro-American authors. 2. Afro-
Americans—Juvenile poetry. [1. American poetry—Afro-American
authors—Collections. 2. Afro-Americans—Poetry.] I. Hudson,
Wade. II. Cooper, Floyd, ill.
PS591.N4P27 1993
811.008 ' 09282 ' 08996073—dc20   92-16034
                                                                      CIP
                                                                      AC

12 11 10 9 8 7 6 5 4 3   3 4 5 6 7 8/9

                Printed in the U.S.A.   44

            First Scholastic printing, March 1993

Contents

Introduction

Poetry, I believe, holds a special place within African-American culture. It is an important part of an oral tradition that has been passed on by our ancestors from Africa. Through this oral tradition, which also includes storytelling and music, history and traditions are kept alive and passed from one generation to another.

Poetry continues to help keep history and traditions alive for African Americans. Written works augment the oral tradition. But many children do not have the opportunity to share in this rich literary legacy. How sad. I am sure many would enjoy and learn from the simple beauty of Langston Hughes's poetry. The eloquence of Gwendolyn Brooks's verse would excite and move them. We must make sure that the work of these great writers is available to children in a format they can understand and enjoy.

That is why I believe *Pass It On: African-American Poetry for Children* is so important. This book not only opens the door of the world of written poetry for young people, it also introduces them to the works of some of our most outstanding African-American writers.

The poems in this collection were chosen with particular care. Each captures a special aspect of the rich African-American experience. There are fun poems, sad poems, silly poems, and serious poems. There are poems of self-affirmation and self-discovery.

Floyd Cooper's wonderful illustrations expand on the meaning of the poems and capture the mood of each while still leaving ample room for the reader's imagination. The illustrations don't overpower the poets' words. Instead, they actually add to their power.

Pass It On: African-American Poetry for Children will be enjoyed and shared by children of all ethnic backgrounds. It is a book for the entire family to share together, from the youngest member to the oldest. Read the poems silently. Read them aloud. Read them alone. Read them as a family. And *pass it on* as others have done before you.

— *Wade Hudson*
1992

5

African Lullaby

Someone would like to have you for her child
but you are mine.
Someone would like to rear you on a costly mat
but you are mine.
Someone would like to place you on a camel blanket
but you are mine.
I have you to rear on a torn old mat.
Someone would like to have you as her child
but you are mine.

— *Traditional*

Dream Variation

To fling my arms wide
In some place of the sun,
To whirl and to dance
Till the white day is done.
Then rest at cool evening
Beneath a tall tree
While night comes on gently,
        Dark like me —
That is my dream!

To fling my arms wide
In the face of the sun,
Dance! Whirl! Whirl!
Till the quick day is done.
Rest at pale evening . . .
A tall, slim tree . . .
Night coming tenderly
        Black like me.

— *Langston Hughes*

Wait Little Joe

"That ditch is too wide," I told Little Joe.
"Thomas is ten, you're only four, you know."

"I can jump that ditch," said Little Joe,
So he pitched himself as far as he could go,
But he missed the mark and landed in the middle!
And he knew at once that he was too little.

Bill fished him out and made him promise
That he wouldn't jump again till he was
                               big as Thomas.

— *Lessie Jones Little*

The Reason I Like Chocolate

The reason I like chocolate
is I can lick my fingers
and nobody tells me I'm not polite

I especially like scary movies
'cause I can snuggle with Mommy
or my big sister and they don't laugh

I like to cry sometimes 'cause
everybody says "what's the matter
don't cry"

and I like books
for all those reasons
but mostly 'cause they just make me
happy

and I really like
to be happy

— *Nikki Giovanni*

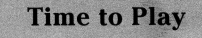

Time to Play

Mama says to play outside.
Wish I had a bike to ride.
I'll fly to the moon instead.
Steer the rocket in my head.
I'll pretend to find a star
no one else has seen so far.
Then I'll name it after me —
        Africa Lawanda Lee!
But for now I'll grab some chalk,
play hopscotch out on the walk.

— *Nikki Grimes*

Jim

There never was a nicer boy
Than Mrs. Jackson's Jim.
The sun should drop its greatest gold
On him.

Because, when Mother-dear was sick,
He brought her cocoa in.
And brought her broth, and brought her bread.
And brought her medicine.

And, tipping, tidied up her room.
And would not let her see
He missed his game of baseball
Terribly.

—*Gwendolyn Brooks*

Daddy's Little Girl

I'm my daddy's little girl.
And my daddy told me,
he borrowed a little piece of sun,
waited until it cooled,
then made me just the way
he wanted me . . .
looking like him
(with a little bit of mommy added).
And that sun he borrowed
is why my face lights up so bright
when I smile,
and why all of me is so sunshiny.

And my girlfriend said
she's her daddy's little girl.
And her daddy told her
he cut her out of some midnight,
with a cookie cutter he got
from her mommy.
He cut her out of midnight,
because that's his favorite,
most fun time.
That's why she is all
of his happiness . . .
especially when she smiles
letting the moon shine,
and the stars flash
across her face.

And my other girlfriend, she said,
she's her daddy's little girl.
And her daddy told her
that he calls her Honey,
because one day he had a sweet tooth.
So he and her mommy gathered up all
the flowers they could,
and gave those flowers
to a whole lot of worker bees.
Those bees buzzed around
and buzzed around,
until they designed her sweet enough
to fill his tooth
with her honey drop kiss . . .
fill his heart
with her honey shined face . . .
and fill his life
with her honey comb smile.

So, my girlfriends and I decided,
our daddies sure went to a lot of trouble
to make us their little girls.
We guess that's why we love them so much.
Thank you God . . . and mommies
for helping them out . . .
We love you too!

— *Lindamichellebaron*

Prickled Pickles
Don't Smile

Never tickle
a prickled pickle
cause prickled pickles
Don't smile

Never goad
a loaded toad
when he has to walk
A whole mile

Froggies go courting
with weather reporting
that indicates
There are no snows

But always remember
the month of December
is very hard
On your nose

— *Nikki Giovanni*

Peas

Peas in the pod
peas in my gut
peas in the belly roll
doing the strut.
Blackeyes over
blackeyes down
blackeyes browneyes going to town

— *Henry Dumas*

17

To Catch a Fish

It takes more than a wish
to catch a fish
you take the hook
you add the bait
you concentrate
and then you wait
you wait   you wait
but not a bite
the fish don't have
an appetite
so tell them what
good bait you've got
and how your bait
can hit the spot
this works a whole
lot better than
a wish
if you really
want to catch
a fish

— *Eloise Greenfield*

18

I Can

I can
be anything
I can
do anything
I can
think
anything
big
or tall
OR
high or low
W I D E
or narrow
fast or slow
because I
CAN
and
I
WANT
TO!
— *Mari Evans*

19

Incident

Once riding in old Baltimore,
    Heart-filled, head-filled with glee,
I saw a Baltimorean
    Keep looking straight at me.

Now I was eight and very small,
    And he was no whit bigger,
And so I smiled, but he poked out
    His tongue, and called me, "Nigger."

I saw the whole of Baltimore
    From May until December;
Of all the things that happened there
    That's all that I remember.

— Countee Cullen

Midway

I've come this far to freedom and I won't turn back.
I'm climbing to the highway from my old dirt track.
      I'm coming and I'm going
      And I'm stretching and I'm growing
And I'll reap what I've been sowing or my skin's not black.

I've prayed and slaved and waited and I've sung my song.
You've bled me and you've starved me but I've still grown strong.
      You've lashed me and you've treed me
      And you've everything but freed me
But in time you'll know you need me and it won't be long.

I've seen the daylight breaking high above the bough.
I've found my destination and I've made my vow;
      So whether you abhor me
      Or deride me or ignore me,
Mighty mountains loom before me and I won't stop now.

— *Naomi Long Madgett*

My People

The night is beautiful,
So the faces of my people.

The stars are beautiful,
So the eyes of my people.

Beautiful, also, is the sun.
Beautiful, also, are the souls of my people.

— Langston Hughes

Harriet Tubman

Harriet Tubman didn't take no stuff
Wasn't scared of nothing neither
Didn't come in this world to be no slave
And wasn't going to stay one either

"Farewell!" she sang to her friends one night
She was mighty sad to leave 'em
But she ran away that dark, hot night
Ran looking for her freedom

She ran to the woods and she ran through the woods
With the slave catchers right behind her
And she kept on going till she got to the North
Where those mean men couldn't find her

Nineteen times she went back South
To get three hundred others
She ran for her freedom nineteen times
To save Black sisters and brothers
Harriet Tubman didn't take no stuff
Wasn't scared of nothing neither
Didn't come in this world to be no slave
And didn't stay one either

And didn't stay one either

— *Eloise Greenfield*

The Voyage of Jimmy Poo

A soapship went-a-rocking
Upon a bathtub sea.
The sailor crouched a-smiling
Upon a dimpled knee.

Young Neptune dashed the waters
Against enamel shore,
And kept the air a-tumbling
With bubble-clouds galore.

But soon the voyage ended.
The ship was swept away
By a hand that seemed to whisper
"No more games today."

The ship lay dry and stranded
On a shiny metal tray,
And a voice was giving orders
That a sailor must obey.

Oh captain, little captain,
Make room for just one more
The next time you go sailing
Beyond enamel shore.

— *James A. Emanuel*

The Dream Keeper

Bring me all of your dreams,
You dreamers,
Bring me all of your
Heart melodies
That I may wrap them
In a blue cloud-cloth
Away from the too-rough fingers
Of the world.

— *Langston Hughes*

The Sand-Man

I know a man
With face of tan,
But who is ever kind;
Whom girls and boys
Leave games and toys
Each eventide to find.

When day grows dim,
They watch for him,
He comes to place his claim;
He wears the crown
Of Dreaming-town;
The sand-man is his name.

When sparkling eyes
Troop sleepywise
And busy lips grow dumb;
When little heads
Nod toward the beds,
We know the sand-man's come.

— *Paul Laurence Dunbar*

Listen Children

listen children
keep this in the place
you have for keeping
always
keep it all ways

we have never hated black

listen
we have been ashamed
hopeless   tired   mad
but always
all ways
we loved us

we have always loved each other
children   all ways

pass it on

— *Lucille Clifton*

About the Poets

GWENDOLYN BROOKS won the Pulitzer Prize for her second book of poems, *Annie Allen*. Among her other published works are *The Tiger Who Wore White Gloves*, a picture book for children; *A Street in Bronzeville*; *Family Pictures*; *Aloneness*; and *Report From Part One*. She is Poet Laureate for the state of Illinois. Brooks lives in Chicago where she continues to write and help other aspiring writers.

LUCILLE CLIFTON is an award winning poet and author. Among her books for children are *Everett Anderson's Christmas Coming*; *Everett Anderson's 1-2-3*; *All Us Come Cross the Water*; and *My Brother Fine With Me*. She teaches at the University of California at Santa Cruz.

COUNTEE CULLEN published his first book of poems in 1925 when he was twenty-five years old. *Color* won the Harmon Gold Award for Literature and established the young Cullen as an important writer during the Harlem Renaissance. Cullen, who wrote such books as *The Ballad of the Brown Girl* and *On These I Stand*, died in 1947.

HENRY DUMAS's poetry has appeared in many periodicals and anthologies. Collections of his work include *Ark of Bones and Other Stories*; *Poetry for My People*; and *Knees of a Natural Man*. Dumas was thirty-three years old when he was killed in 1968 by a policeman on a Harlem, New York City, subway platform.

PAUL LAURENCE DUNBAR's first volume of poems, *Oak and Ivy*, was published in 1893 when he was twenty-one years old. He achieved national recognition with his third book, *Lyrics of Lowly Life*, which was published in 1896. Dunbar helped to launch a new era in African-American literature that began in the early twentieth century. He died in 1906 when he was thirty-four years old.

JAMES A. EMANUEL is the author of several volumes of poems, including *The Treehouse and Other Poems* and *Panther Man*. He is also the author of a biography of Langston Hughes and is the co-editor of *Dark Sympathy: An Anthology of Black American Literature*. He lives in Paris, France.

MARI EVANS is an educator, writer, and musician who resides in Indianapolis, Indiana. Formerly Distinguished Writer and Assistant Professor, ASRC, Cornell University, she has taught at universities around the country. Evans is the author of numerous articles, four picture books for children, and four volumes of poetry. She edited the highly acclaimed *Black Women Writers (1950–1980): A Critical Evaluation*.

NIKKI GIOVANNI was born in Knoxville, Tennessee, and graduated from Fisk University in 1967. She has written many books, including several for children. They include *Spin a Soft Black Song*; *Ego Tripping and Other Poems for Young People*; and *Vacation Time*. She is one of the most notable writers who emerged during the 1960s.

ELOISE GREENFIELD is the author of more than twenty books for children. Her biographies, fiction, and poetry have received numerous awards. Some of her books include *Darlene*; *Talk About a Family*; *Nathaniel Talking*; *Grandpa's Face*; *Under the Sunday Tree*; and *Night on Neighborhood Street*.

NIKKI GRIMES is the author of books for young people such as *Something On My Mind*; *Growin'*; and *Poems By*. Her poems, articles, essays, editorials, and photographs have appeared in *Essence* magazine, *Cricket* magazine, and *Collier's Encyclopedia Year Book*.

LANGSTON HUGHES was one of America's most prolific writers. For more than forty years he wrote novels, collections of short stories, plays, newspaper columns, children's books, and many volumes of poetry. *The Dream Keeper*; *Montage of a Dream Deferred*; and *The Panther and the Lash* are just a few of his published books. Hughes is still considered by some to be the dean of African-American writers. He died in 1967.

LINDAMICHELLEBARON, also known as Linda Dudley, is an author-educator-performer who conducts workshops for teachers, parents, administrators, and students. *The Sun Is On* is her most recent book of poetry.

LESSIE JONES LITTLE wrote three books for children, including two with her daughter, Eloise Greenfield. Her last book, *Children of Long Ago*, was published two years after her death in 1986.

NAOMI LONG MADGETT was born in Norfolk, Virginia, but grew up in East Orange, New Jersey. The author of seven books of poetry, including *Star by Star*; *Exits and Entrances*; and *Octavia and Other Poems*, Madgett founded Lotus Press, a publishing company located in Detroit, Michigan. She is also professor emeritus at Eastern Michigan University.

FLOYD COOPER

FLOYD COOPER was born and raised in Tulsa, Oklahoma. He received a degree in fine arts from the University of Oklahoma. After working for a greeting card company, Mr. Cooper moved to New York City to pursue a career as a children's book illustrator. In 1988, his first book, *Grandpa's Face*, by Eloise Greenfield, was named an ALA Notable Book for Children. Among the books he has illustrated since are *Chita's Christmas Tree* and *The Girl Who Loved Caterpillars*. The artist now lives in Parlin, New Jersey.

WADE HUDSON

WADE HUDSON is a writer whose published works for children include *Jamal's Busy Day*; *AFRO-BETS® Book of Black Heroes from A to Z*; *Beebe's Lonely Saturday*; and a play, *Freedom Star*. In 1988, he and his wife, Cheryl, founded Just Us Books, a publishing company that specializes in books for children that focus on the African-American experience. They live in East Orange, New Jersey.

Acknowledgments

Every effort has been made to trace the ownership of all copyrighted material and to secure permission to reprint these selections. In the event of any question arising as to the use of any material, the editor and the publisher, while expressing regret for any inadvertent error, will be happy to make the necessary correction in future printings.

We thank the following for permission to reprint the copyrighted materials listed below:

Gwendolyn Brooks. "Jim" copyright © 1956 by Gwendolyn Brooks Blakely. Reprinted from *Bronzeville Boys and Girls* by Gwendolyn Brooks by permission of HarperCollins Publishers.

Lucille Clifton. "Listen Children" copyright © 1987 by Lucille Clifton. Reprinted from *Good Woman: Poems and a Memoir, 1969–1980* by Lucille Clifton by permission of BOA Editions Ltd.

Countee Cullen. "Incident" copyright © 1925 by Harper & Brothers; renewed 1953 by Ida M. Cullen. Reprinted from *On These I Stand* by Countee Cullen by permission of GRM Associates, Inc.

Henry Dumas. "Peas" copyright © 1989 by Loretta Dumas and Eugene B. Redmond. Reprinted from *Knees of a Natural Man* by permission of Thunder's Mouth Press.

James A. Emanuel. "The Voyage of Jimmy Poo" copyright renewed 1989 by James A. Emanuel. Reprinted from *Whole Grain: Collected Poems, 1958–1989* by permission of the author.

Mari Evans. "I Can" copyright © 1976 by Mari Evans. Reprinted from *Singing Black* by Mari Evans by permission of the author.

Nikki Giovanni. "The Reason I Like Chocolate" and "Prickled Pickles Don't Smile" copyright © 1980 by Nikki Giovanni. Reprinted from *Vacation Time* by Nikki Giovanni by permission of William Morrow and Company, Inc.

Eloise Greenfield. "Harriet Tubman" copyright © 1978 by Eloise Greenfield. Reprinted from *Honey, I Love* by Eloise Greenfield by permission of HarperCollins Publishers. "To Catch a Fish" copyright © 1988 by Eloise Greenfield. Reprinted from *Under the Sunday Tree* by Eloise Greenfield by permission of HarperCollins Publishers.

Nikki Grimes. "Time to Play" copyright © 1991 by Nikki Grimes. Reprinted by permission of the author.

Langston Hughes. "My People" and "Dream Variation" copyright © 1926 by Alfred A. Knopf, Inc. and renewed 1954 by Langston Hughes. Reprinted from *Selected Poems* by Langston Hughes by permission of Random House, Inc. "The Dream Keeper" © 1932 by Alfred A. Knopf, Inc. and renewed 1960 by Langston Hughes. Reprinted from *The Dream Keeper and Other Poems* by Langston Hughes by permission of Random House, Inc.

Lindamichellebaron. "Daddy's Little Girl" copyright © 1981 by Linda Michelle Baron. Reprinted from *The Sun Is On* by Lindamichellebaron by permission of the author.

Lessie Jones Little. "Wait Little Joe" copy right © 1988 by Weston Little. Reprinted from *Children of Long Ago* by Lessie Jones Little by permission of Philomel Books.

Naomi Long Madgett. "Midway" copyright © 1957 by Naomi Long Madgett. Reprinted from *Star by Star* by Naomi Long Madgett by permission of the author. "Midway" first appeared in *Freedomways* magazine in 1957.

Special thanks to Lauren Stevens, our editor at Scholastic Inc., for helping to make this book a reality.